Yesterday's Moon

A Father's Account in Verse of Growing Up in the West

Gaynor Dawson

iUniverse, Inc.
New York   Bloomington

Yesterday's Moon
A Father's Account in Verse of Growing Up in the West

iUniverse books may be ordered through booksellers or by contacting:

iUniverse
1663 Liberty Drive
Bloomington, IN 47403
www.iuniverse.com
1-800-Authors (1-800-288-4677)

ISBN: 978-1-4502-4972-0 (sc)
ISBN: 978-1-4502-4973-7 (ebook)

Printed in the United States of America

iUniverse rev. date: 08/09/2010

Yesterday's Moon

Nothing feels as warm as the hearth back home,
With all the smiling faces on the wall.
When I reach the day, that I don't need this my pay;
I'm going to pack my things and leave it all.
I'll find my way back to some small town
And see if that old moon is still around.

The moon comes up here almost every night.
It looks just as big and it shines just as bright.
It goes through the phases, quarter, full, then new;
And sometimes it's silver, and sometimes it's blue.
But I don't feel the mystery that was such a treat,
Shining through the tree tops, up on Newton Street.

Maybe I took too long coming to this place,
Maybe it's the footprints now left upon its face;
Whatever the reason, it's not like it was back then,
And I long for the day when I'll feel that way again.

The seasons pass here, just as in my youth:
Summer's bounty yields to winter's bitter truth.
The fragrance of the fruit still hanging from the trees
Is carried on the cold air of every morning's breeze.
Pleasant as it is, it doesn't smell as sweet
As the grapes in the vineyards surrounding Newton Street.

Maybe it's the sniffles I seem to get each year
Maybe it's exhaust fumes from all the traffic here.
Whatever the reason, it's not like it was back then
And I long for the day, when I'll smell the grapes again.

The leaves change colors here, just before the snow.
They shimmer in the light, when the fall winds blow.
They drift down to the earth and skitter through the yard
Where they hunker in the garden, as winter sets in hard.
They gather in the corners and crunch beneath my feet,
But they don't sound the same as they did on Newton Street.
Maybe with time's passage, my hearing's lost its range

Maybe leaves are different, with all the climate change.
Whatever the reason, it's not like it was back then
And I long for the day, when I'll hear that sound again.

It snows here every winter in great big lacy flakes
Just like the ones that used to come from over by the lake.
They drift into a blanket that sparkles in the sun
And brighten up the night, when the day is done.
I lay myself upon them and wave my hands and feet,
But the angels aren't the same as they were on Newton Street.

Maybe I've grown so much that I've lost my youthful form,
Maybe all the chimneys here make the snow too warm.
Whatever the reason, it's not like it was back then
And I long for the day, when they'll look that way again.

Blue Mountain Mornings

Blue Mountain Mornings*

Morning comes early to Mt. Wilson's peak.
Later in the valley it finds Joseph Creek.
After sliding down ridges and over the scree
The time has come for its daily decree
Let it be known all along the way:
Here comes a glorious Blue Mountain day.
And if, down the road, things don't turn out right,
It's morning again in a day and a night.
Morning returns in a day and a night.

It's morning, and daylight chases the dark
From the last coyote to the first meadowlark.
A plaintive good-bye, a joyous hello,
While the earth is bathed in the dawn's early glow.
The fragrance of bunch grass, yarrow, and pine
Lifts off the hills in the warm sunshine.
And if, in the end, it doesn't feel right,
It's morning again in a day and a night.
Morning returns in a day and a night.

It's morning, and the skyline is framed in black lace,
As the limbs of the sumac reach out to embrace
A horizon transformed by softening shades,
When the day is a promise that is yet to be made.
The sights and the sounds let all senses partake
Of the beauty of an earth that is coming awake.
And if, in the end, they don't blend out right,
It's morning again in a day and a night.
Morning returns in a day and a night.

It's morning, and the sun's reddish hue
Shines like a ruby in each drop of dew.
The moon and the stars ever westward march,
Chased by the day from their heavenly arch.
While earthbound shadows, reluctant to go,
Hide in the canyons where chokecherries grow.
And if, in the end, the shades are not right,
It's morning again in a day and a night.
Morning returns in a day and a night.

It's morning, and the whisper within the trees
Is the sound of the wind as it dances with leaves.
Beckoning the sun to come into view
And transform the night from ebony to blue.
Dawn's muted tones become vibrant and strong,
Painting the land with their visual song.
And if, in the end, the music's not right,
It's morning again in a day and a night.
Morning returns in a day and a night.

Evening comes early along Joseph Creek.
Later the shadows climb Mount Wilson's peak.
It's there that the sun's last bright golden rays
Crown one more glorious Blue Mountain day.
The gorge gathers darkness, chasing the light,
As it settles into the velvet of night;
No matter what happens along the way,
It's evening again in a night and a day.
Evening returns in a night and a day.

*This verse was originally written about the Blue Mountains
of Washington and Oregon. It has since been edited to
describe the Blue Mountains of New York and recorded
by Carmen Gilman. In so doing, she has turned a fond
remembrance into a beautiful song.

Indecision

Sleep and dreams held me in thrall,
Until some event I can't recall.

What time it was, was hard to say,
For the mist and clouds that awaited the day
Kept the signs that the sun was on its way
To a gradual change from black to gray.

There'd been no moon to pierce the night,
No planets or stars burning bright,
Just shapeless forms, more black than white,
Their edges blurred in the meager light.

Morning was an impressionist's design
Of shaded pools without angles or lines;
So its meaning could only be divined
Within my heart and not my mind.

I had retired with decisions to make
And the burden of knowing what was at stake
Had rendered me somewhat reluctant to take
The journey from aware to fully awake.

I lay there for hours, or so it seemed,
Balanced on the narrowest of beams.
Dividing my conscious thought from dreams,
Unable to commit to either extreme.

On opening my eyes, it was only to see
That I was surrounded by the monotony
Of the grayness that had overtaken me,
And stretched for a seeming eternity.

Mocking me firmly as if on parade
Was every decision I'd never made;
Cards I was dealt but left unplayed
Taunted me from that formless shade.

But I clung to belief that change was due,
The clouds would part, the sun shine through
And awakened by the vibrant hues,
There would be no doubt what I should do.

Having put the decision beyond my reach,
I closed my eyes and returned to sleep.

A Winter's Tale

Winter lay hard in the ground from the remnants of
December's last storm,
When the opens came drifting back in, looking for a place
that was warm.
They looked good given the conditions, except for the fifty-
first
Who must have just calved, for her bag was nearly burst.
The night sky was crystal clear, the air was sharp as a knife;
If someone didn't go find him, that calf would forfeit its life.
Shorty milked the old cow until a bottle was overflowing
In hopes they'd find that slick in time, to get him up and
going.
The young hands were eager to finish, heard the holiday
calling their names.
But three old timers just saddled up, said all nights were
about the same.
The herd had been up on the north side, in the timber on
Starvation Ridge.
And they pointed their horses toward the Dipper, to use what
light it could give.
After two grim hours of searching, their efforts had come to
no good,
So they turned back to the east where they knew an old line
shack stood.
It hadn't been used in years, but the spring-fed stream in the
back
Kept the grass green much longer, so a cow might pause
there to calve.
Since the night had grown much colder, it was with great
surprise
That they looked down in the swale and saw a new hole in
the ice.
"Cow must have gone out on the pond, weighing more than it
would allow.
Little chance we'll save this calf, he's bound to be frozen by
now."
But you don't give up 'till you're certain, so they rode down
the icy track
Only to see that there was someone moving around in the
shack.

They were miles from the nearest road. It was a place
someone might hide.
So there wasn't much positive thinking about what was going
on inside.
They dismounted in a hurry, tied the horses off by the creek,
Slipped up to where the slats were loose, in hopes of getting
a peek.
The flames from an open fire had the shadows dancing wild,
In contrast to a silent young couple that stood there holding
a child.
Their clothes were torn and soaking wet, their journey had
been tough,
And to three old saddle-worn cow-pokes, it was pretty
powerful stuff.
Little question the infant was newborn, had just arrived that
night,
He'd been washed clean with snow melt and dried in the
fire's light.
While lying there beneath them, beside the open flame
Was the calf the boys were seeking, and he'd been treated the
same.
Earl knocked on the ramshackle door, then opened it a crack,
Said, "Folks, you'll find a warm bunkhouse just a couple of
miles back.
We need to get that little doggie along by his mother's side.
You're welcome to join us there; if you don't mind a bit of a
ride."
The couple just shook their heads, said it was time to get,
Had an uncertain destination, but knew they weren't there
yet.
Those old timers just stood there, struck by the simple truth;
Seems they all had felt the same, at some time in their youth.
One by one, they sidled back to where the horses stood,
And searched for old things that might do the folks some
good.
One brought an old horse blanket, one brought some dried-
out meat,
While the third had but tobacco to lay at the father's feet.
No other words passed among them; they gathered up the
calf
Fed it part of the bottle, left the family with the other half.
There was a sense of urgency in the horses' returning gait,

Like they were all barn sour and hadn't the patience to wait.
But instead of holding the horses back, the riders spurred them on,
Intent on reaching the main ranch before the night was gone.
One stopped down in a meadow to chop the first tree he could get,
Then drug it in behind his horse on the end of his lariat.
The leader turned to the others and drawled as he did:
"Been smiling all the way back, just thinking about that kid.
Heck of a way to come into this world, but I got this funny hunch;
Of all the children born this night, he'll be the best of the bunch."
His companions only nodded, but each had a similar thought,
As they joined the younger fellows and shared the tree they'd brought.
Over the years as they looked on, not sure what they would see,
They had no way of knowing just who that child might be;
But to the man they thought that their little band
Had been there for the arrival of a new top hand.

Every Place Has Two Horizons

Every place has two horizons
Where the earth meets the sky:
One where the day begins
And one where it goes to die.

The east is filled with promise,
As the sun's first rays of light
Warm the waiting world
And break the gloom of night.
So red sky, to the optimist,
When seen at break of day
Is just another rose,
To smell along the way.
Yet, morning can be contrary,
When pursued in eager flight.
It shortens up the day
And hastens on the night.

The challenge is to balance
What the two would have us see
And draw our own conclusions
About the red sky's prophesy.

The west, it seems, is so different,
For to chase the setting sun
Is to prolong the current day,
Leaving time to get more done.
And yet it feeds the pessimist
As the approaching end of day
Gives rise to melancholy
For the hours that slipped away.
Unfulfilled, but good intentions
Give rise to sad regrets
And red sky foretells darkness
When the sun finally sets.

But despite all their differences
They are forever bound,
For we find the one we don't pursue
Still there when we turn around.
And chase them as we might,
Through experience we divine,
That it is our destiny
To live between the lines.

The Ghost of Mt. Wilson

We sat around the camp fire
On many an autumn night,
Poking at the embers
As our fantasies took flight.

We'd gaze up at the stars
In those vast western skies
And seek a higher truth
By swapping harmless lies.

It never seemed to matter
That the game that got away,
Grew ever more impressive
With the passing of each day.

We'd laugh and carry on
Until someone made a toast
To the legendary buck
Known as Mt. Wilson's ghost.

He was a massive mule deer
Beneath a trophy spread
That resembled a rocking chair
Mounted on his head.

Seems everyone had seen him,
And from the tales they told,
He clearly did get around,
And he was mighty old.

His good health was credited
To uncanny guile and speed;
But because he was bullet proof,
Long life was guaranteed.

At least that was our story,
For back in those young times;
We were all great marksmen,
If only in our minds.

It was that immortality
That preyed upon us most.
Nothing stayed around that long,
Except perhaps a ghost.

But I am here to tell you
I know with certainty;
That he was made of flesh and blood
Just like you and me.

It was late into October
And few had bagged their buck,
When Dad and I set out one day
To try and change our luck.

Dawn had broken cold and crisp
Beneath a pale white sun
And everywhere we chanced to look
Deer were on the run.

We were a bit too eager.
We jumped out of the car
And emptied out our rifles
From a little bit too far.

The deer kept right on running,
In defiance of our will;
Despite all of the mortal wounds
We'd inflicted on those hills.

And so it went all morning,
Our bad luck didn't change.
We saw a lot of deer, but they
Were just beyond our range.

By noon it had become quite clear
It would take a sacrifice
And climbing up Mt. Wilson
Would have to be the price.

The backside is six thousand feet
Of rock and talus slide,
Interlaced with brushy draws
Where deer and elk will hide.

So we climbed up the lava chutes
In that spare and rugged land,
And thereby placed our ante
For the day's one final hand.

Tired, but ever watchful,
We topped the final rim;
And before I could catch my breath,
We both had spotted him.

As in the campfire stories
We shared on all those nights,
He stood there like a statue
In the day's fading light.

A quick sprint down a side draw
And slow crawl up the slope
Had me within a stone's throw,
And that monarch in my scope.

That's when it flashed before me;
If I put that trophy down,
What would we have to talk about
When next year came around.

He would remain forever
As he was that very day,
And all the myth and mystery
Would simply fade away.

There'd be no room to speculate
On his point count or its spread,
Just measurements of everything
That grew upon his head.

The decision was an easy one,
When I realized after all,
That a living legend far outweighs
His head upon my wall.

And now it is contentment
That joins me in the camp,
On those cold autumn evenings
That conclude the daily tramp.

It's with a knowing smile
That I listen to the tales,
And wait for the time to come
When silence should prevail.

Then I rise to my feet
And offer up this toast:
My ode to the legend
We call Mt. Wilson's Ghost.

Dayton And Dick

Dayton and Dick loaded their grips
And went searching for Klondike gold.
Leaving wife and kids in what was their bid
To get rich before they got old.
From Frisco's Bay up to Skagway
They took berths on the Native Lass,
The rest of their stake, bought what it would take
To make it over Chilkoot Pass.
Then they turned north to the Yukon's source
And the treasure that lay in its bed.
But when they were there, the river was bare
And they learned why the horse was dead.

They had the fever. They followed their dream.
Of a fortune lying at the bottom of the stream,
Shining them on like the harbor lights,
Calling their names like the wind in the night.

They'd had it in mind, gold was easy to find,
The nuggets would glow in the sun.
But there was no glow, just ice and snow
And a lot of hard work to be done.
So they carved up the land, sluiced it and panned,
Finding little more than despair.
And on that sad note, they returned to the boat
With nothing to pay for their fares.
Dick sang and danced, while Dayton washed pans
And they worked their way back home,
Only to find, the wife left behind
Dropped the kids and fled on her own.

It was a deep lesson from a shallow dream,
Seeking their fortune at the bottom of a stream,
It was Elmo's fire, not the harbor lights,
And it left them with nothing but the wind in the night.

Dayt made his way down to Monterey
Where his success was finally won
Raising apricots that looked a lot
Like nuggets that glowed in the sun.

To raise his brood, Dick farmed too,
But ultimately died from a cold
Caught in a creek 'neath Lassen's Peak
Where he searched for Sutter's gold.
He'd wander alone and bring rocks home
To see if gold lay within.
But truth be told, when one bore gold,
He couldn't recall where he'd been.

So two brothers started with the very same dream.
Seeking their fortune at the bottom of the stream.
One learned that gold sheds a frigid light,
The other found treasure round the hearth at night.

He shared that wealth with his nephew as well,
That was my Dad; this is his tale to tell.

Only Faith Can Make it Rain

He was born and raised on a hard luck Western farm,
Where the struggle to survive often hid the native charm.
A builder, and a dreamer, a farmer through and through,
He couldn't think of anything that hard work couldn't do.
But he was sorely tested the first time he found out
The price of a good year was five more of drought.
So it was early in his life when he came to understand,
The bane of his life was finding water for the land.

He dug ditches to bring the snow melt down from the hills;
Then fashioned canvas dams to spread it through the rills.
He flooded fields daily, but the job was never done
Most of his water went out as tribute to the sun.
The fields proved quite fertile 'til one year by and by,
When there was no more snow and his ditches all ran dry.
The once green carpet of young wheat turned brown in only
days
Then disappeared completely when it all had burned away.

He searched all around for where water might be found.
If not from up above, then perhaps deep in the ground.
He traded in his ditcher for a hollow auger drill
And found a buried river that drained the distant hills.
But he mined out more water than moisture ever fell,
So he chased the water table to the bottom of his well.
When he could drill no deeper, the plants began to wilt
And wheat turned to straw on the farm that he had built.

With his pockets empty and the fields now tinder dry,
He knelt and bowed his head, vowing to make one final try.
He borrowed enough money to pay for one crop more
Then prayed the clouds would come and beat the banker to
his door
That banker was a fast one, but just not fast enough
With a mighty clap of thunder, the heavens opened up
And chased him back to town with a wall of tiny drops
That blessed the dried out earth with a golden bumper crop.

It takes good seed and soil to grow a crop of grain
And both of those abound out upon the plain.

But just those two alone, won't get the groceries grown
Without water all the work will be in vain,
And in the arid West, despite man's very best,
We've learned that only faith can make it rain.

Geronimo

A few years ago at a conference, I heard a fellow speak
About where he got his paddles when he was up a creek.
When he was in the Navy as a pilot years before,
He'd been shot down and captured in the Vietnam War.
Then sent to the Hanoi Hilton for a regimen of terror,
With endless days to wonder was he ever leaving there.
He'd used the time to make a list, in case he did survive
Of all the people whom he credited with keeping him alive.

Topping the list was the airman who'd packed his parachute,
For without that skillful work, this story would be moot.
But the plan for his descent hadn't ended in his cell,
That was just the preview for a journey straight to Hell.

Now fortunately for him, he never took that trip,
Thanks to other parachutes he found within his grip.
Throughout his life, his family, his coaches, and his friends
Had molded him into someone who was able to transcend
The daily pain and horrors that his captors would instill
In their many failed attempts to break this pilot's will.

I admired his outright courage and the witness that he bore
To the impact of his mentors those many years before.
While his captors truly thought that he was lying there alone
He was in fact accompanied by a support team of his own:
Folks who had inspired him and given him the grit
To hold on to his sanity while the guards assaulted it.
When he refused to leave until the enlisted men went free
He was using another parachute, while packing one for me.
You see from time to time, my life has dropped me in the void
And just before I crashed, a parachute deployed.
Someone in my past had prepared it, most certainly not I,
Sensing I would need one, without knowing when or why.

It wasn't just the lessons, but how they had been taught
That ensured their basic values didn't go for naught.
They showed me the importance of doing something right;
How working hard all day helps you sleep all night.
The associated pain need not your spirit break,
If the focus is the end point and not the path you take.

Eventually, I realized there's no reason I can't teach
Survival skills to others who might be thrown into the
breech.
Now, I won't by nature stand aside while others join the fray;
So the parachutes that I provide are packed in my own way.
They are woven out of threads that I have gathered from
hindsight,
Like if you want to help folks win, you join them in the fight.

Those who lead by example always carry greater weight
Than the fellows in the stands who just pontificate.
So I fold the lines and silk, and then I climb on board
Where I can demonstrate just when to pull the cord.
I recommend to others that they take a similar line;
Leading from the front, not just prodding from behind.
For experience has taught me there is little one can gain
From the guy who yells Geronimo, but never leaves the plane.

Werganserland

Werganserland

Just a little ways out of town, where the pavement turned to sand,
We discovered another world that we called Werganserland.
It was nestled beneath an old canal that supplied a few homesteads,
But the water had been diverted and the fields were parched and dead,
Save for a few ornamentals that had found water deep below
And were hardy enough to continue, where only sage could grow.
The structures were long since gone, their remnants widely strewn,
While desert glass, like lupine, blossomed in the nearby dunes.

It was small as kingdoms go, for the parental constraints at play,
Required we return by dinnertime at the end of every day.
So the boundaries were prescribed as the distance we could walk
When leaving in the morning and returning by six o'clock.
But acres aren't the metric by which greatness can be gauged
For this was hallowed ground where many a battle was waged
To thwart the forces of evil we had discovered gathering there,
As they plotted their foul intentions on a town that was unaware.

It wasn't a wealthy kingdom, so our treasury made do
With return deposits on pop bottles as our only revenue.
While steady as an income, the net was not a lot
For searching all the side roads left us dry and hot,
And a handful of shiny coins was difficult to ignore
When cherry phosphates waited at the soda shop next door.
So our armory consisted of many a strange creation
From what we found along the way and our wild imaginations.

The folks we saw from time to time were singularly

disinclined
To see anything but desert out beyond the city line.
And so it was our duty to stand alone and form the shield
Against an enemy disguised as the creatures of the field:
Ground squirrels and jack rabbits in the service of some dark lord
Quickly surrendered to the power of our trusty wooden swords.
So off they'd run in disarray, vanquished by our might,
But to return next weekend and resume the epic fight.

It wasn't until much later, our eyes now opened wide,
We regretted having not chosen to fight on the other side.
Despite our young conviction, time has erased all doubt,
The animals weren't moving in, the town was moving out.
Laboratories and offices have grown like metal weeds
With roads and pipes and power lines, to serve their every need.
There are ball fields and tennis courts, a trail where people jog,
But not a trace to indicate that two boys and a dog
Had once reigned benevolently over a vast expanse of sand
That was a mighty kingdom they called Werganserland.

Mountain Roads

On a logging trace in the West Cascades
When I was eight years old,
It seemed back then, round every bend,
Was a story to be told.
We moved real slow with our voices low;
We thought we'd see some game.
We meant no harm and we went unarmed;
Had a safari just the same.

That's the joy of a mountain road.
It takes you where you want to go.
Even if you seek to find,
A place that's only in your mind.

There were ten switchbacks to the Big Chewack,
From up on Billy Goat Pass.
And we soon learned they're frightening turns,
When you're low on brakes and gas.
But to three young bucks in a pickup truck,
The answer was easy to see:
Just close your eyes and think real wide;
Leave the rest to gravity.

Whenever I go down Crow Creek Road
And see the distant hills,
Their rugged slopes give rise to hopes
I'll never get my fill.
I feel the breezes, smell the trees;
I hear the eagle's cry.
But it's always true, there's too much to do;
So it's just in my mind's eye.

Life's flown by to the point where I
Know more than half mine's gone.
And despite my best, I must confess
There are roads I've not been on.

And though it's plain, that will remain
I pray for at least one more.
For I've a mind, that you have to climb
A mountain road to heaven's door.

So when life becomes a heavy load
It's time to take another mountain road.

Bobber Watching

The old man sat back in the shade, where the riverbank was cool,
Quietly watching a bobber floating in the languid pool.
He had an air of expectation for some undefined event,
Despite a posture that belied little more than self content.

A young boy sat beside him just as he did most every day,
Recording it all in his memory and faithfully storing it away.
But his was not a body easily committed to repose,
He had the look about him of someone standing on his toes,
As his eyes darted repeatedly to the water down below,
Intent to see if something would take the bobber under tow.

There was a smile on the old man's face as he crafted his replies
To questions circling round the boy like a swarm of little flies.
The first query was always the same, but it still would bring a grin:
"Grampa, is today the day that old catfish cashes in?"

The old man hesitated as if choosing what to say
Then repeated the time worn story he recited every day.
But he made little changes and their impact was profound,
To the point where every day their discussion broke new ground.
It sat astride the decades that formed the old man's past
And the future that was lurking where the bobber had been cast.

He was like a master weaver who heard within his head
Voices that directed him on where to place each thread.
The result was a fine work of art, whose subtle truth was made
Along about the time when the day's light began to fade.

Then the old man gave a shout, as he tried to save
His dignity and the cane pole from a cold and watery grave.
Just as suddenly it seemed to them, when he had it under grips
The line went limp in his hands and the catfish kept his chips.

The old man told the boy it'd be a shame to just give in
And solemnly they vowed that they would come back once
again.

He gave the boy a knowing look as they were homeward
bound,
Bemoaning all the other times that luck had let them down.
The boy went off to do his chores, the old man to wash his
hands,
Where he glanced into the mirror that graced the basin
stand.

"Thank you" he said quietly, "for another perfect day."
Knowing the time was coming when he'd no longer get away
With keeping the boy from getting close enough to look
And realize his grandfather never did bait up the hook.

Working away in the barnyard, the boy was lost in thought
Of how he'd keep from letting on his granddad had been
caught.
For he had known instinctively since he could first recall
That when they went to the river, they weren't after fish at
all.

My Old Shirt

I did my hunting in the hills and my fishing from the shore,
Dressed in an old wool shirt from Dawson's Dry Goods Store.
It was just a hand-me-down, but woven in its plaid
Were the remnants and reminders of my outings as a lad.
Many were the starlit nights with only the ground for my bed,
I'd roll up that old wool shirt as the pillow for my head.
The cool evening breezes, the sound of a mountain stream,
And the smell of the day's encounters, filled my head with
dreams.

It was a little too thin for the coldest winter storm,
And in the midst of summer, it was a little too warm.
It was frayed and it was faded, it was torn and it was stained,
And there were no two alike of the buttons that remained.
But I loved that shirt and I lived in fear,
If it ever hit the wash, it might just disappear.

My rambling days were numbered, of that there was no
doubt
When I met a dark-haired beauty, I could not live without.
There was nothing I'd refuse her, including my last name,
'Til she borrowed that old wool shirt and caused my world to
change.
It was just a shirt to her and no harm was intended
When she returned it to me as something washed and
mended.
I saw the anger in her eyes when she heard my sudden gasp
And lost, in that moment, both my future and my past.
It was a little too clean for the lifestyle that I had
And the lemon-fresh smell almost drove me mad.
It had been frayed and faded, now it was cleaned and
patched.
Up the front and on the sleeves, every button matched.
I had loved that shirt and much as I had feared,
After one trip to the cleaners, it had just disappeared.

In this life there are rainbows, so during all this pain,
I found its mate in Mom's closet and my life began again.
It was a little worse for wear, but woven in its plaid
Were the remnants and reminders of days spent with my

Dad.
It wasn't mottled gray, it was forest green and red,
And in place of elbow patches was a clutch of broken threads;
But every time I smelled it, my heart was filled with hope,
For in all those aromas there was no hint of soap.
It's a little too thin for the coldest winter storm,
And in the midst of summer, it is a little too warm.
It is frayed and it is faded, it is torn and it is stained,
And there are no two alike of the buttons that remain.
Now I love that shirt and this vow I have sworn:
It never will be washed, as long as it can be worn.

Just So Stories

There's a book on the shelf
In the room down the hall
That I haven't read,
Since I can't recall.
But the stories on the pages
Ramble through my head,
When I close my eyes
Every night in bed.
The characters are fanciful
The morals simple truth,
But they seemed so profound
In the sunshine of my youth.

I learned of a place
Where kangaroos don't hop;
Rhinos had thin skin,
And leopards had no spots.
Where Strong Heart was a dog
Whose steadfast bravery
Sent him through the forest
Saving little boys like me.

The book is well worn now;
The binder glue is cracked.
The letters have all faded,
In the front and down the back.
But if I rub my finger
Where they once had been,
I feel the great adventures
That wait for me therein.
They take me back in time
To the comfort of the knee,
Where I sat in wonder
As they were read to me.

I learned of a place
Where kangaroos don't hop;
Rhinos had thin skin,
And leopards had no spots.
Where Strong Heart was a dog

Whose faithful bravery
Sent him through the forest
Saving little boys like me.

It was with great surprise,
One day when I was blue,
To open up that book
And not find the words I knew.
The stories were familiar,
But not all that profound
And when it came to Strong Heart
He was nowhere to be found.

I guess it was my father
And not Kipling long ago
Who wove the dreams together
That made my world Just So.

Apparently Not

A few years back, fate revealed to me
What seemed at the time, just a novelty.
Some fellows had built a little machine
That could take a chicken and pluck it clean.
Not the sort of thing you'd use every day,
Unless a flock of chickens came your way.
And as a cattleman, I was ready to bet
That a bucket of wings was as close as I'd get;

But, apparently, I was wrong.

One day, for reasons that I can't explain,
We bought a hundred chicks along with grain.
They were cute at first, all fluffy and round,
Then feathers grew out in place of their down.
Now I was convinced, that with some luck,
We could buy that machine and have it pluck
All those feathers and quills and such
(After all, it couldn't cost much);

But, apparently, I was wrong.

Demand was high or the supply was spare,
Or maybe it was made from something rare.
Whatever it was, the price was too grand
So we looked to pick those birds by hand,
When Jeff got to thinking (not a good sign)
And disappeared out back for quite some time.
He returned to announce we were ready to start,
With a plucker he'd made from a bunch of old parts;

But, apparently, he was wrong.

He'd put baby bottle nipples on a rolling pin,
Then a belt and a motor to make it spin.
After hot water baths for every bird,
We'd rev the engine till the motor purred.

Then the whirling nipples were brought to bear
And feathers starting flying everywhere.
Now, it wasn't too long before I came around,
To thinking we'd be done before the sun went down;

But, apparently, I was wrong.

Oh the feathers came off by the multitude;
With some quality control, those birds were nude.
So many plumes flew in a short time span
You'd have thought a pillow had hit the fan.
Then things slowed down to a lower gear
As parts of nipples started to appear.
We'd assumed that babies were tougher than chicks
And those nipples could handle a pretty good lick;

But, apparently, we were wrong.

That rolling pin had been stripped down clean
And we had no spares for our machine.
Now once you've started on a hundred wet hens
There's no waiting 'round to begin again.
At that point you can only conclude
That technically speaking, you've been screwed.
That's the point at which I came to understand
I'd been sentenced to pick those birds by hand;

Unfortunately, this time I was right.

Most stories from the farm have a moral or two.
This is no exception, when properly viewed.
In fact, some folks find an obvious one,
Don't count your fryers before they're done.
Others say it refers to best laid plans
Or something related to a bird in the hand.
But after eating feathered birds all year long,
Those Chick-fil-A cows have it wrong.
For me, the message should be written in stone
Eat beef and leave those chickens alone.

Some of the Best Days*

Nothing stirs this soul of mine
Like a mountain breeze and the smell of pine.
It takes me back to the lofty trees
And the cold water of the Little Naches,
With emerald pools and lively falls;
Rapids slashing at the canyon walls;
A pond reflecting summer skies
Shattered when the cutthroat rise.

    Some of the best days I ever had,
    Were days spent with my brother and dad,
    Chasing memories with a rod and reel,
    Saving the best in a wicker creel.
    Releasing little ones back to the stream
    So they could fulfill tomorrow's dream.

My father and my brother and me,
Were like a pod with just three peas:
Identical creases in our Stetson hats,
Leather puttees worn like spats,
Canvas pants and wool plaid shirts
Frayed throughout and stained with dirt,
Gentle souls in hardened cases,
With all day smiles on sun-burned faces.

It was early morning when we awoke
To the smell of bacon and campfire smoke.
Three miles back and the hike was done
To wet our lines in the first good run.
Sometimes they'd strike and sometimes not,
But it never mattered what we caught.
It was all about being and being there,
Sharing the feeling that hung in the air.

    Some of the best days I ever had,
    Were days spent with my brother and dad,
    Chasing memories with a rod and reel,
    Saving the best in a wicker creel.
    Sometimes I wish I too were small;
    So they'd throw me back to relive it all.

*John Kirk, a wonderful fiddler and folk singer, has put this piece to music in what is now a wonderful tribute to the pleasures of fly fishing.

Monster Nights

Three of us shared a room when my pajamas had feet;
To this day it's a wonder we got any sleep.
As tired as we were after stories and prayers,
We revived by the time the folks were downstairs.
It would start with a giggle or a sound in the hall
Or maybe a shadow that danced on the wall.
There'd have been no harm had it ended there;
That wasn't enough to bring parents upstairs.

Their return was the product of an enterprise
In the form of a game that we had devised.
My crib in the middle was a stone between shores;
The trick was to cross without touching the floor.
And that simple task was our ruination,
For success always brought a celebration.
That and the bouncing to prepare for a leap
Didn't sound much like children asleep.

With all that commotion, what we had in store
Was father's stern voice at the bedroom door.
But his deep furrowed brow wasn't able to hide
The kindred spirit he harbored inside.
Try as he might, he couldn't disguise
The merriment dancing there in his eyes
Bemused or not, the game was through,
As sleep came calling for the other two.

Now, we'd riled a monster with all of that noise
And I was quite certain it ate little boys.
The others didn't know what was at stake,
So the burden was mine to keep them awake.
I'd ask them a question or beg they recite
Something so long it would last through the night.
But after a while, they closed their eyes
And left me alone to improvise.
That's when I decided it was probably a troll
And wouldn't hurt much if he swallowed me whole.

Fearing I'd wake in a wet, smelly place,
I pulled up the blanket to cover my face
And tucked in the edges all about,
While holding my breath until I passed out.

After hearing this story, some folks disagree,
They say there's no way that it's about me.
For I'm known to doze off and sleep like a stone
Long before my body is ever prone.
So I simply tell them the story is right;
I'm still making up for those long monster nights.

The Stand

Elk hunting was a privilege given Dad's sons,
At the time of maturity 'round age twenty one,
When we had the time, the need and desire
To trade urban living for a place at the fire.
Each year in November, the first full week
Found us deep in the woods above Rainbow Creek,
Where the elk liked to graze and gather around,
Before trailing on up to their wintering grounds.
We in turn watched over each new band
From a spine of basalt we called the stand.

The serious hunter neither moves nor talks,
Sitting motionless on a stand as if one of the rocks.
And that's how it was for Jeffery and me,
If we alone crouched 'neath that tree.
But Dad's presence brought other factors to work
In which harvesting game was only a perk.
Had he mounted rewards from his hunts back then
His soul would have hung from the wall of his den.
He wasn't after ribbons for taking first place;
He lived for the joy of just running the race.
He was there for the time he spent with his sons,
And success never hinged on the firing of guns.

If he got hungry, he proceeded to eat,
And when it was cold, lit a fire for heat,
Regardless of the impact it might have on game
When they smelled the food or noticed the flame.
Now much as we protested those comforts he sought,
I can't think of a time that it cost us a shot.
To the contrary, the numbers made it quite clear,
He outperformed everyone year after year.
When despite all the odds he'd succeed in the end,
He'd laughingly credit God's pity on old men.
But even in seasons when the elk moved away,
 We were always enriched by the end of the day.
We'd see the night skies turned coral with dawn
Transition to cobalt as the day passed on.
We'd watch a clear night devour the day
Leaving nothing behind but the Milky Way.

Sometimes the earth was a frozen tableau
When storm clouds came early with December's snow;
Straining for the sounds of hoof beats near by,
We'd hear flights of swans passing high in the sky;
And the symphony of brush strokes played by the trees
As the wind had its way with their limbs and their leaves.

Throughout it all, we hunters three
Were one little thread in a tapestry.
But the two of us boys instinctively knew
The art would be lost if that thread went askew.
We were in training to anchor the line
And offer up hope for those far behind.
We were guardians of something we couldn't define;
But had to pass on in the goodness of time.
Sadly, the mission became all too clear
When Dad passed away in the summer one year.

He'd shown us a beacon to cut through the gloom
That we couldn't discard in that hospital room.
So we carried his ashes to the places he'd found
Like the draws in the Blues where the elk bedded down.
The next time I sat there all wrapped up in wool,
Ostensibly waiting for a shot at a bull,
I felt him beside me and knew right away
Trophies and meat weren't the prize that day
Much to the shock of my then grown son
I broke hunter etiquette, as my father had done.
I forsook the stillness and reached to extend
My hand for the torch in that world without end.

The thread is intact, unbroken and true,
Maintaining the image as if it were new;
Despite dwindling numbers of game on the land
The real prize is waiting at a place called the stand.

Stairway To Heaven

When I was in my twenties, I never did commit
The kind of youthful sins that might cause me to forfeit
My place in heaven, but it wasn't guaranteed,
So I took out some insurance by the doing of good deeds.
I coached the parish boys in how to dribble right
And advised the high school youth every Sunday night.
But my brother was a vestryman, earning better scores,
So he found it rather easy to entice me to do more.
He promised me wings for sure, if I'd help a week or two
By reroofing the church's annex: a job long overdue.
I thought the timing set a quite ambitious goal,
But agreed in an attempt to save my mortal soul.
Seems I never paid attention Sunday mornings in my pew
To just how steep that roof was and what you'd have to do
To stay alive and upright as you covered each bare spot,
With rows of brand new shingles far above the parking lot.
The irony was (as so often with these things)
It would have gone much faster, had they issued us those
wings.
We tied tethers around our waists so as to prevent
Any but the shortest of uncontrolled descents.
It was in midsummer when hot shingles start to flow,
Which limited our work to when the sun was low.
As you might imagine, those conditions tied our hands
And work did not progress in accordance with our plans.
Given our regular jobs, time quickly passed us by
So on Sunday evenings, I advised youth from on high.
The kids sat on the lawn to hear all about faith and hope
As I illustrated the concepts, while dangling from a rope.
When we finally finished, the pastor was content,
But I rather doubt the effort will ensure I'm heaven sent.
Given my intervening years, it's probably a better bet
That climbing that church roof is as close as I will get.

Morning Prayers

Patience is a virtue
That you might not find,
With a cold eight year old
In a duck hunting blind.

Many was the Sunday
I made the search,
After successfully evading
Another day in church.

We'd get up in the dark
And dress from head to feet
With everything we thought
Might preserve body heat.

It was a wonder we walked
With all the clothes we'd donned;
It might have been faster
Had Dad rolled us to the pond.

But he was the soul of patience,
And the greatest of his joys
Was taking to the fields
With his spaniel and his boys.

After breaking out the ice
We'd set the decoys up.
Then pack in that blind:
Three hunters and a pup.

And that's when my plans
Started to unwind
'Cause there wasn't any way
To stay warm in that blind.

After centuries of hunting
The rules are the same;
No one moves 'til they shoot
And the dog gets their game.

So I'd pray for the sun
To thaw that arctic sky
Then I'd pray we'd see a duck
Fool enough to fly by.

Now you must see the irony
With what I had to do.
For I was there by virtue
Of not being in my pew.

But with Dad's six-day week,
It was catch as catch can,
And fortunately for us,
God's a family man.

So Sunday was for hunting,
And I relied on prayers
To keep the warmth from seeping
Through all those layers

Yet I kept getting colder
As I tried to sit still
And the numbness in my fingers
Slowly robbed me of my will.

In time Dad took pity
And declared the day through
While each boy claimed
A deeper shade of blue.

Then as if by magic
It seemed we could fly
As we raced to the car,
And turned the heat up high.

We'd barge into the kitchen,
To tell Mom of our luck
And all the fun we'd had,
While waiting for a duck.

Now that might seem confusing
On days that were bleak;
But Sunday church was coming
In just another week.

Jefferson And Me

Like two shooting stars in the August night,
Brothers and best of friends,
We'd ride out each morning,
To see what was beyond the bend.
Troubles were one more challenge
For free spirits like us two,
And laughter was a way of life;
The only way we knew.
A couple of outlaws without crime,
Two mavericks running free;
Life is a grand adventure,
For Jefferson and me.

Whether cutting wood or stretching wire,
It was always one on one
Competition to the final stroke,
Not caring who had won.

When the laughter has subsided
And its time for the final ride,
Something tells me with certainty
He'll be there by my side.
We'll walk up to the golden gates,
Knock twice and wait to see
Which way they send hard cases,
Like Jefferson and me.

He knew me better than I knew myself
And he took me by the hand.
He led me through my boyhood
And what it was to be a man.
He loves my kids as he loves his own
And offers selfless care
He does his best to fill their needs
When I cannot be there

So it will not surprise me
As they review our separate slates,
When I am sent the other way
And he's passed through the gates.

Though surely it will break my heart,
 I can only thankful be;
For the many years of joy they gave
To Jefferson and me.

Tuna Can Hockey

When we were young and thought we'd live forever,
My brother and I each would endeavor
To slide a tuna can between two rocks
On a pond that lay just up the block.
The minute the ice would begin to form,
We'd put on everything we thought was warm.
From coats and shirts to quilted long johns;
We could hardly walk with all we had on.
Then we'd pull out of some packing crates
Four hand-me-down women's figure skates.
Fortunately, we both had skinny feet,
Since they were our cousin's, and she was petite.
We'd pull and we'd push and we'd scrunch up our faces
Until we could fasten those tattered laces.

As much as it hurt, the pain in our toes
Would quickly be gone as soon as they froze.
Then we'd hobble to where the willows grew thick
And break off a couple for hockey sticks.
There was no need for choosing sides,
So we went right out to center ice.
Up went the sticks, down went the can
And that's when the joyous riot began.
We'd beat on each other from head to toes,
But not feel a thing through all those clothes.
And whenever the can was hit in the fray,
It was a break-neck sprint to where the goal lay.
Scores were made but not recognized,
For this was about demons being exorcised.

The harder we hit and fell on the pond,
The closer we got, and the stronger our bond.
There's something to be said for a good cross check,
Even when you're the one lying on the deck.
We'd slash and skate and defend our half,
But mostly we'd sprawl on the ice and laugh,
'Til darkness chased us back up the street
For a bite of dinner and a little more heat.

There were times when others would join in the game,

But no matter how few, it was never the same.
Team matches had passes and polite little duels,
Along with the nuisance of following rules.
It was exercise, not catharsis, and truth be told,
I could get plenty of that without being so cold.
And whatever the team that I had been on,
When I stepped off the ice, the demons weren't gone.
Heading home those times, we never understood
Why we weren't as warm or the food quite as good.

We still get the urge on cold winter days,
To find some good ice and hit away.
But the knees are too sore to strap on the skates,
So we verbally joust in endless debates.
Folks look on in wonder, for they are denied
A glimpse of the images playing inside
Of two boys battling with sticks in their hands,
To capture the joy from an old tuna can.

Murphy and the Badger

Murphy loves a good story;
So on his behalf,
I'll tell this one where
A badger got the last laugh.

It took place years ago
On the eastern slopes,
Where Murphy and some friends
Were scouting antelope.

Murph's dad had drawn a permit
And to improve Ken's luck
The boys had offered to help
Locate some trophy bucks.

They loaded all their camping gear
Into Ken's new SUV
Then headed out of town
On a back road Odyssey.

It was early when they got there,
So they stopped to glass around
When they spied this big old badger
Digging a hole in the ground.

One of the guys got thinking
It might be kind of neat
To shoot and stuff that badger
As a stool for his feet.

It took but a single shot
To put the beast away,
So they tossed it in the back
For skinning later that day.

They climbed back in the rig,
Their prowess now intact;
As Murphy fired the engine up,
There was a ruckus in the back.

Murph knew before he looked,
But registered disbelief;
When a glance in the mirror
Revealed a mouth full of teeth.

Lethal looking claws churned
Beneath that white-striped head,
The foot stool was joining them,
Looking anything but dead.

Now a Badgers' temper is complete
Its fury has no bar.
So the boys took little time,
In abandoning the car.

And there out on the prairie,
Four doors open wide,
Sat the car with engine running
And the badger safe inside.

Once they were beyond the reach
Of the badger's vicious bite
They had a chance to laugh,
And get the story right.

The aim may have seemed good,
But lethal it was not,
For they had but stunned the prey
With that single shot.

And now the thrill of victory
Tasted of defeat,
As the badger got all comfy
Nestled in the driver's seat.

He poked his nose knowingly
At the instruments on the dash,
Until Murph began to fear
He might do something rash.

What if he engaged the gears?
The thought gave Murph a chill;
With that engine running,
A wreck lay down the hill.

Murph reckoned they could end it all
By shooting it again;
But no one wanted to return
A shot-up car to Ken.

The badger seemed contented,
As if it was all planned,
And he was clearly enjoying
Having gained the upper hand.

With his point firmly made,
He finally stepped on down
And strutted up the hill,
To his hole in the ground.

Not another shot was fired,
At the badger's calm retreat.
The boys were content to leave
Despite their clear defeat.

All would tell the story
Each in his own way.
You'd wonder if the stories
All happened that same day.

But on just this one point
Everyone agrees;
That badger'd still be driving
If he'd found the brake release.

Wild

They were called the Hidden Lakes
But we knew where they lay;
And we went there in the summer
For a chance to get away.
It was fifteen miles of hiking
Through snow-clad rocky peaks,
Over two mountain passes,
Carrying provisions for a week.
They were nestled in a valley,
Where fir trees cloaked the land;
And they sparkled like four sapphires
On a single silver strand.
The campsite sat between the lakes,
But we were tired and sore;
So we'd stop and fish the first,
To whet our appetites for more.
Adrenaline now flowing,
We'd find a second wind
To shoulder up our packs
And hit the trail again.
I could feel the tension easing,
As my soul was reconciled
To the beauty all around me
That was primitive and wild.

Next morning we would head out
To the furthest shining jewel,
Carrying nothing but our tackle
To resume the annual duel
With the legendary trout
In those waters cold and deep
That had beckoned us so early
From the comfort of our sleep.
If we managed to stay quiet,
Upon the mountain air
We'd hear the loons' strange laughter,
For they too were fishing there.
We'd build a driftwood raft
To ply the lake's contours
And drag the pristine waters

With a pocketful of lures.
We'd peer into the depths
For signs that would betray
The presence of the denizens
That brought us there that day.
When everything was perfect
Those lunkers were beguiled,
Into risking all for something
That looked, but wasn't, wild.

And when there were no fish,
Day's end was our reward,
As the shadow of the mountains
Climbed up the eastern shore.
Sounds became more muted,
So too, the colors and light,
As the world was slowly ceded
To the Kingdom of the Night.
I'd watch the dippers circle,
Around the polar star,
As meteorites lit up the dark
Like fireflies in a jar.
Sometimes in the distance
A sudden storm would break,
Lightning raced across the sky
And the ground began to shake.
I 'd lie there mesmerized
As trees were torn asunder,
Flames would dance across the ridge
Accompanied by the thunder.
Only now in retrospect,
My sensations all compiled,
Have I begun to appreciate
That symphony so wild.

The four lakes still lie hidden
In that valley far away,
And if I took the notion,
I could drive there in a day.
Yet I haven't been for decades;
I've gone on to other things,

As time and circumstances
Trimmed my fledgling wings.
Now, if chaos finds me,
Or life seems all too tame,
I weigh the urge to return
Against the risk it's not the same.
What if the force of Nature
Or what some would call progress
Has transformed the wild beauty
Of what once was wilderness?
I will not take the chance
There is substance to my doubt;
My pack remains unloaded,
And I take the safer route.
By wandering through my mind
To where the memories are filed,
I'm transported to the wilderness
When the wilderness was wild.

Just For The Joy Of It

Just For The Joy Of It

Cattle ranching isn't easy and gets harder every day
As prices go down for calves, and up for fuel and hay.
The pleasures of working stock struggle to compete
With all those other things required to make ends meet.
Days in the saddle where the deer and the antelope play
Have given way to meetings with a herd of CPAs.
Seems it took something special to jog my memory
As to why I was convinced that this was the life for me.
But I had that very epiphany just the other day
As I rushed to get some cows moved up across the way.

I was out making repairs with that old dog of mine
When I noticed that my cattle had gathered up the line.
I thought if I just set the gates, I could ease them through,
And spare myself a rodeo that would cost an hour or two.
I had the gates wide open and was working them myself
When Cassie got the notion that I could use some help.
She went after the closest one, snapping at her heels
And in the blink of an eye she had them racing through the fields.
I hollered just as loud as I could 'til they were all long gone,
But it seems the dog assumed I was cheering her on.

While it's possible she's now too deaf to hear commands at all,
I think that in reality she's learned to screen my calls.
Be that as it may, when she had finished up her run,
She came racing back beside me to attest to all the fun.
Her eyes were sparkling bright above a hound dog smile
As though she was a pup again, if for a little while.
She was dancing round my ankles, merry as can be,
Oblivious to the frustration building up in me
And that's when it hit me like a bolt down from the blue
There was a simple reason for me doing what I do.

For I knew in that moment what set me on this course:
It is the mountain trails beneath the rhythm of a horse.
It 's watching newborn calves when they first hit the ground,
As they struggle to their feet and start to bounce around.
It's early morning sunshine, cold, but full of hope
And the pride of picking up two with a well-worn rope.
It's the simple acts of living on and off the land
Where the health of the herd is the best measure of the man.
And so I know with certainty that I never will resign
For the very same reason as that old dog of mine.

I'll keep chasing cattle, just for the joy of it.

Gathering

It was a rule during roundup, despite the gnawing pain,
Cowboys couldn't stop to eat, till the horses had their grain.
So they were groomed and saddled, and well into their hay,
Before I saw the biscuits that would fuel my coming day.
That left little time before the horses yearned to run,
Eager to take me down the ridges ahead of the rising sun.
The forest was a masterpiece in all the shades of night,
That burst out in full color with the onset of early light.
The dogs ran at my horse's heels ready to herd the steers,
Until they had a chance to practice chasing hapless deer.

We were all in it together, the horse, the cow dogs, and me
Gathering cattle in the canyons, loving life and living free.
And I thought that I was in heaven, with no idea how I got in,
But I sure was glad that I had; it beat anywhere I'd ever been.

Birdsong filled the air as they wakened to the day,
For they too were gathering, with winter on its way.
I rode up the rugged slopes almost too steep for trees
Then led the horse down again, in deference to his knees.
I had my lunch in a pocket, drank water from the spring
Fresh air was the mountain's gift: I'd no use for other things.
Long hours at an easy pace would end in a sudden rush,
When a maverick would break out through the underbrush.
Then as the shadows lengthened, all hands met up again
To push the herd up the trail and into the holding pens.

We were all in it together, the other cowboys and me,
Longing for a warm fire and some homespun company.
And I thought that I was in heaven, with no idea how I got in,
But I sure was glad that I had; it beat anywhere I'd ever been.

Wrapped up in my bedroll, it didn't seem so strange
That my neighbors all so stubbornly resisted any change.
I listened to the water's music, as I lay beside the stream
Uncertain if I was still awake or caught up in a dream.
I watched Orion stalk his prey across the endless skies
And fought impending slumber so as not to close my eyes.
I heard a great horned owl, somewhere beyond the springs
And thought I knew just how he felt soaring on his wings

Then weary from my day, I slipped beneath the veil
And let my mind return to the magic of the trail.

We were all in it together, the stars, the sky and me
Lost in a cosmic dance that played on silently.
And I thought that I was in heaven, with no idea how I got in,
But I sure was glad that I had; it beat anywhere I'd ever been.

Many a year has passed now, since last I rode those hills,
Or slept out in the open unaffected by the chill.
Now it is my fervent prayer, no matter where I've been,
They'll come for me the same time they come gathering all
men.

An Uncivil War

I irrigate my pasture with water from a lake
Where the inhabitants begrudge every single drop I take.
It seems their ambition is to be creatures from the deep;
So they've found a crew to shore up every little leak.
Now in the spring I find myself adding to my chores
The necessary measures for the annual beaver wars.

The inlet is a perforated pipe over thirty feet long;
So nowhere down its extent should the flow feel strong.
But those devious little rodents found it in a day
And vowed to prevent me from taking water away.
They signaled their intent to make a war of it
By starting up construction without posting their permit.

They scooped the bottom mud into a covering mound
So that after several days, my pipe could not be found.
Back up in the system, the pressure simply died
And I couldn't pump much water, no matter what I tried.
As I waded into the lake, new violations were revealed:
Any certification they had should have been repealed.

I dug out my pipe, then installed some metal stakes,
Attaching iron grates with which a cage to make.
Now surely I'd have water, for it looked in all respects
The cage was far too wide for those dam architects.
Imagine my chagrin, when after weeks went by,
While looking at my sprinklers, I saw them all run dry.

Seems Bucky and his kin had gathered limbs from trees
And added from the shoreline a mix of more debris.
This they wove into the grate, as high as two feet tall;
So the cage that I had built was now a wooden wall.
Then mud was plastered on, making it so tight
It prevented any water from getting to my pipe.

Deconstruction was mighty hard with all those sharpened sticks
As I waded in the mud that was now knee-deep thick.
I kept sinking lower, until the water reached my nose
In order to keep breathing, I was standing on my toes.

When a flat tail spanked the water just behind my back,
My obituary changed from "drowned" to "heart attack."

I plotted tactics every night to spring on them each day
While the beavers worked their midnight shift just the other way
They met nightly at their lodge hoping to bring online
Some crafty innovation in their overall design.
I hesitate to mention that there was a part of me
That could not but admire their ingenuity.

However, recent happenings have made it all too clear
There's an uncivil element in those little engineers.
For now they've added bioweapons to their standard load
That on occasion sends me to my bed or the commode.
Indignity demands that I respond in kind
And final resolution is now forming in my mind.
My plan is really simple to defeat those swimming rats
I must convince the world to wear more beaver hats.

Back In The Day

There were two tons to an acre when we had good yields
Laid out in ragged lines across the dusty fields.
The stacker rode the wagon, loader walked 'long side,
Bucked the bales on the bed, stacked 'em four bales wide
Three tons on the wagon, was the best we did back then.
We'd drop them in the barn, just to stack them up again.
It was never ending work, but if you needed hay
That was how it was done, back in the day.

It always got too hot before the work was through
Because we couldn't start 'til the sun dried the dew.
And if storms were brewing, we worked faster yet,
For each bale seemed a ton, when it was soaking wet.
And wet bales would smolder until a fire broke,
Then all our summer labors would go up in smoke.
There was no time for idleness if you needed hay,
That was how it was done, back in the day.

When the heat was at its peak, we made it less severe
By thinking of the time when machines were priced too dear.
When pitch forks put the burden on our ever-aching backs
To get the hay up high where the thatcher wove the stack
And by the end of those days, we'd lay upon the trailer
And dream of better times when we could buy a bailer.
So the memories of harder times helped along the way
By reminding us how far we'd come, since before the day.

Now sometimes late at night, I'd feel my body yield
To the pleasures of recovery from working in the field,
I'd dream of new machines to buck and load the bales
And do the heavy work that making hay entails.
It often made me wonder, if the price tag weren't too tall,
Would I lie in bed and never feel a thing at all?
So I went on making hay staying with the time worn ways
And thanked my lucky stars to be living in the day.

Cowboy's Lullaby*

In the midst of the winter, 'neath a sliver of moon
The north wind rises and picks out a tune
On barbed wire fences stretched banjo tight
By the fruit of my labor and the chill of the night.
The notes sound lonely, but before too long,
A distant coyote joins in the song.
And my heart is beating in time with the sound
Of my horse's hooves on the frozen ground

I 'm riding high where the eagles fly,
Where the Oregon Mountains touch the sky;
Where the sun and the rain
Are the simple refrain
In a cowboy's lullaby

The moonlight dapples the tall western pine
As they sway in the breeze just to stay in time.
And the horse's hot breath in the frigid air,
Flows like a mane of ghostly white hair;
A million stars glitter above and below,
Like diamonds dancing in the fresh fallen snow.
Hoof prints draw a line from where I've been;
And soon they will lead me back home again

The night seems colder as I top the rim.
So I turn up my collar and pull down my brim.
There are miles to go with more of the same
But I'm already feeling the home fire's warm flame.
So a flick of the reins, a shift of my weight
And the horse is flying through the old wooden gate.
The works never done, but that's all right
I'm lost in the music; I'm part of the night.

The unfettered freedom of the northern night
Lifts my spirits and puts them to flight
Swooping down canyons and over the ridge.
Life is a river and I am a bridge
From the past to the present and around the bend,
Here in the land that stands on end.
Where the music is magic and flows in a stream

Eroding the lines between life and a dream

I 'm riding high where the eagles fly,
Where the Oregon Mountains touch the sky;
Where the sun and the rain
Are the simple refrain
In a cowboy's lullaby

The journey's well worth it, no matter how long,
For I am a cowboy and this is my song.

*This poem has been put to music and is sung using the
second verse as a chorus.

Dugan

There was a time when I was a cowboy
And I spent my youthful days
Riding high up in the mountains,
Rounding up the strays.
Horses were my only companions,
So of necessity,
I broke twenty or thirty
And a few of them broke me.
The good ones were a blessing.
The bad made me the fool
But the best of the worst by far
Was Dugan, my brother's jack mule.
He was sixteen hands, if he was an inch
Out of a single-foot mare.
He was also single minded,
And the trouble started there.

I started training that renegade jack
The minute he hit the ground.
I put on my best halter
And let him lead me around.
I gentled him with a steady hand,
But he never did quite tame.
I worked his feet most every day,
But it only honed his aim.
I let him run free for his second year,
Far off in the rugged hills.
It put strong legs under him
And an even stronger will.
So it wasn't Dugan I sought that day,
As the sun shone bright and clear
Early one August morning
With the pens full of maverick steers.
I put him into the milling herd,
Trying to cut out culls,
Only to find the alley
Was filled with a monster bull.

Dugan! Dugan! What you gonna do?
That bull is tearing up the earth and coming after you.

Dugan! Dugan! It's the last time I'll ride you.
If you're not fast,
We'll never last,
And you'll be gloves and glue.

He was an ornery, sullen beast
And quickly made it clear,
The only way he was moving
Was to run us out of there.
He lowered his head and mounted a charge,
Snorting and kicking up mud.
Old Dugan stood there half asleep
With no intent to budge.
The earth shook beneath his feet
When Dugan spun to kick.
He caught the top of that bull's head
And dropped him like a brick.

The wide-eyed steers fell silent,
As the bull lay on the ground
Then opened up his eyes to search
For the beast that had put him down.
But there was no Minotaur
No rival mean and cruel;
Just one pale, white old cowboy
On top of a sleepy mule.
'Twas just a day in the life of that mule,
But the bull was never the same.
He'd seen a source of power
That put his own to shame.
There wasn't a thing that bull wouldn't do
To stay in front of that jack,
No matter what the cowboy did
While hanging on Dugan's back.

Dugan! Dugan! What you gonna do?
That bull is tearing up the earth and coming after you.
Dugan! Dugan! Although we almost died,
The truth be known,
From this day on,
You're the only critter I'll ride.

Post script: This is a true story. Duggan was sold a few years later to a mule trainer who soon had him winning shows throughout the Northwest. Dugan was retired in his twenties and last heard was enjoying being put out to pasture.

Leonard

His hand slid out of mine as he left his mortal shell
And, if some folks have it right, descended straight to Hell;
But that's not a conclusion with which I can agree;
For how could he have been that bad and yet so good to me?

Leonard lived a simple life; there was little he desired
Beyond a view of mountain peaks, and a warm place by the
fire;
A horse to go the distance when he was on the brand;
And a life whose story was revealed by looking at his hands.
They were tough as drying leather; they were dark as the soil
From years of countless days in what seemed like endless
toil.
A portion of his finger tip was gone from being shorn
By one too many dallies around his saddle horn.
His knuckles were a battleground, where abrasions did
abound
From stacking hay and pulling wire when gloves could not be
found.
The joints were often swollen and bent to ease the pain
From far too many hours spent holding frozen reins.
But they were strong and willing hands, many were their
deeds,
And they were always able to fill his simple needs.

He was rough as they come, his language rougher still;
So after one encounter, many felt they'd had their fill.
For they lacked the patience; you had to wait him out
To discover that a whisper lay just beneath the shout.

Leonard loved his way of life, and never seemed to tire
Of gazing at the wilderness or deep into the fire.
He'd take a moment's rest in the shade of ancient trees,
And seem to find more strength with each new passing
breeze.
He loved to hear the sandhill cranes heading north to nest,
And feel the power of the wind as a storm gave out its best.
The sleepless nights of calving time, put a sparkle in his eye
As he watched each new arrival , while its mother licked it
dry.

He loved to stare up at the stars late into the night
And see the great expanse of space glitter with their light.
He'd hear the sound of thunder out across the plain
And weigh the threat of wildfire against the hint of rain.
But even if no single drop caressed the bone dry slopes,
He was grateful for the chance that gave rise to all his hopes.

It was hard to see him lie indoors and gasp for his last breath,
And hear him cry defiantly, just before his death.
Some said it was contrition for living a life of sin,
I think it was his testament for never giving in.

There were always basic needs beneath my great desires;
So Leonard helped me separate the smoke from all the fire.
He made me look on each new day to see what it would bring
And be thankful for the gifts therein disguised as simple
things.
We shared a common pride from challenges well met;
While he railed against excesses that left me deep in debt.
I learned success was sweeter when I worked my own way
out;
But his hand remained extended in case I suffered doubts.
And though he has passed on now, I feel his presence still,
In my growing self reliance and my ever stronger will.
I see with sharper focus that as my life proceeds
There can be greater pleasure in fulfilling simple needs;
Like stopping for a rest before the journey's end,
And telling all who'll listen that I was Leonard's friend.

My Place By The Fire

And so my day begins.

By morning I have managed to move myself around
So my body can conform to the contours of the ground.
My bed roll's wrapped up closely, hoping to delay
The loss of warmth I'll need to make it through my day.
I linger in the blankets and try to hang on tight
To fragments of the dreams that came to me all night.
There is a calm contentment in deferring deliberately,
The cold wind and hard work that lie in wait for me;
But tendrils of the campfire smoke soon drift into my lair
And find the lurking hunger that I feel growing there.
The promise of hot food is all that is required
In league with need and duty, together they conspire
To put me into motion, seeking my place by the fire.

And so my work begins.

The sun slowly fades and I must come to grips
With the day's residue now in my back and hips.
Morning's welcome motions too often were repeated
Such that my reserves have long since been depleted.
There is a low and nagging ache in my fingers and toes
As the heat of my exertion slips out through my clothes.
The shadows coalesce to finally bring the end of day,
So I loosen up the reins, and let the horse find his way.
My thoughts race out ahead of me to a time when I can feel
The flames dance upon my skin as I sit before my meal.
Alluring as it is, I know that my chores must be done prior,
So at least for the moment, duty trumps desire,
Before I can sit down, reclaiming my place by the fire.

And so my work ends.

The sun now has reached a point that seems so far away
As the void of the heavens steals the heat from the day.
I can sense but not see something moving on the plains
And find myself drawn closer to the light and the flames.
But it isn't long before the firewood runs its course
And the recipients of the warmth have now become its

source,
As we talk amongst ourselves, we share the burdens of the day
In a communion that also serves to keep the night at bay.
But in the end we're weary as our bodies can attest,
And they cry out for relief that can only come from rest.
By that time the merry flames have finally expired,
I can no longer set aside the nagging need to retire.
I return to my bed roll, relinquishing my place by the fire.

And so my day ends.

Shorty and Slim

Shorty and Slim were side kicks
And they were thick as thieves;
But it wasn't clear what bound them,
Since they never could agree.

Their opinions were as far apart
As were their natural heights.
Shorty believed at the end of the tunnel,
Was a lantern shedding light.

While Slim was a doubting Thomas.
And what kept him alive,
Was knowing that Shorty's lantern
Was the oncoming Nine O'Five.

So as you might imagine
They had very different views
Of pretty near everything
That happened 'tween the two.

Shorty blamed Slim's negativity
On thin air at his height,
While Slim was just as certain
Shorty said things just for spite.

So it came as no surprise one day
As dark clouds filled the sky,
That Shorty smiled in wonder
As Slim turned a jaundiced eye.

"As usual Slim, you've got it wrong
You're too hungry for the feast.
Just roll up your collar and see
There is beauty in this beast.

"Remember just last winter
Those drifts that blocked the sun,
Were made of tiny snow flakes
That fell gently one by one.

"And the torrent of the spring flood
Choked with silt and trees,
Was but myriad tiny raindrops
Returning to the sea."

"That's nonsense," Slim cried in disgust,
"Put your poetic thoughts away.
And let me describe to you
Your true part in this play.

"When clouds cover the mountains,
And rain and hail fill the sky;
When the sound of the wind blowing
Is like a train going by;

"When the thunder booms so loudly
That it shakes the very sod;
Even the shortest cowboy
Looks a lot like a lightening rod."

Now that only made Shorty laugh,
Though there was truth just the same.
"Why I'd be the Electric Horseman
With my fifteen minutes of fame."

Slim was singularly unimpressed;
Said if he was to keep herding cattle
By golly it would be on a short horse
That was equipped with a rubber saddle.

And so they went on bickering
Throughout their working days
Views colored by the lenses
Through which each fellow gazed.

People became accustomed
To those quite different views
To the point they now describe them
Just like those buckeroos.

So when half full seems right
When one describes the cup,

That means a view like Shorty's,
And things are looking up.

But when it seems half empty,
The distance from the brim;
Why that's quite another matter
And things are looking Slim.

The Windmill

Not long ago, I slipped out of town
And rode into the hills to look around
For a little bit of tranquility
And a haven from the demons that pestered me.

I hadn't been out too long alone
When my mind took off on a trail of its own.
I got the notion that it would be grand
To just stay out there and live off the land.

I'd wander about for fish and game;
Maybe gather berries and grow some grain.
I'd listen to the wind instead of cars
And fall asleep by counting stars.

I was lost in the vision when I crested a hill
And found myself staring at an old windmill.
It looked like a sentinel covered with rust,
As it stubbornly guarded fifty acres of dust.

A gust of wind had it turning full out,
But no drop of water graced the spout.
I could sense the frustration of years of toil
And feel the pain plowed into the soil.

I could see the tears in despairing eyes,
As they searched across those cloudless skies.
The rattle of vanes made it all too clear:
I wasn't the first to want to live here.

The sun and fresh air give it allure,
But it's draught and storms you must endure.
When water comes, it falls as snow,
Then it's too late, and crops won't grow.

I shook the image and headed back in,
Leaving the mill as it sang in the wind.
Don't get me wrong, the dream's not lost,
But I've a better sense of what it might cost.

So I'll bide my time and blend instead
Both the past and present for what lies ahead.
After all, if Paradise were so easily found,
Everyone would move there and they'd call it a town.

Tractor Therapy

I was in the back pasture when something caught my eye,
A patch of should-be grass with thistle four feet high.
At what I pay for feed these days, I was quick to realize
I needed to do something to cut those weeds down to size.

And with all of the problems in the beef industry,
It seemed to me the time was right for some tractor therapy.
So I grabbed some collateral and headed to the bank
Intent on a loan to fill my fuel storage tank.

No matter how they lace it with those fancy marker dyes,
Fuel still costs a king's ransom for all us regular guys.
But I needed enough power to make the outcome clear,
I'd trump the thistles play with my old mower and John
Deere.

It took but an hour to mend an air leak in the lines,
Another one or two and the hydraulics worked just fine.
So I pulled up to the brush hog, primed and ready to go
When I remembered a little problem with my PTO.

The last time I had an implement hitched to my three point,
I'd broken a number of splines on the takeoff coupling joint.
My equipment is too old and badly mishap prone;
So buying the right replacement would take another loan.

I was out of collateral and had to pass on that card,
So my play was an option to mine the scrap metal yard.
And like all good ranchers, I had a monstrous pile
Of everything that ever broke or just went out of style.

Certainly, somewhere in there was just a perfect match
That would aid me in my battle with that pesky thistle patch.
First I had to clear a path through piles of pure refuse,
So that I could focus on the things that actually fit my use.

Down near the bottom of the pile, from my long retired 8N
Was a coupler that looked to me like it might work again.
It was frozen to a shaft with a broken threaded pin,
But after drilling with an easy out, I was eager to begin.

The spacing was still wrong, but the spline count was just right,
So I fashioned up a set of shims that made it fit real tight.
Then I cleaned out the supply bins hoping to retrieve
Something I could fashion into a protective sleeve.

It was half a roll of duct tape and it added silvery flair
In turning a slap dash fix into a permanent repair.
Poised then to fire the engine, it was with some dismay
I realized that my efforts had consumed my entire day.

I did my daily chores as the horizon swallowed the sun
And congratulated myself on all the work that I had done.
I left the tractor in the barn and homeward made my way,
Thinking to myself that I'd had quite a day.

And as I passed the field, I noticed with a sigh
There were thistles growing freely, four and a half feet high.
I made a mental note to mow them someday if I could,
Thinking some tractor therapy was bound to do me good.

Waiting for Winter to Be Gone

The nights get shorter with every passing day;
The sky a little bluer as the clouds blow away.
Sunshine, like a blanket melts away the chill
When it finds me napping by my window sill.
I wake up thinking that spring's back again
And rush to the door to usher it in.
But there's only disappointment waiting for me there
For I am cut to the quick by a blade of frozen air.
It's back to the fire to put another log on
And count down the hours until a warmer dawn.
Nothing's changed since fall
But the calendar on the wall,
And I'm still waiting for this winter to be gone.

There's hardly any hay on the stack in the shed,
And each new calf 's another mouth waiting to be fed.
So I keep my eye out for any sign of graze
And stare into the sun as it burns away the haze.
The snow's melted back now, there's little to be seen
And if I strain hard enough, I sense a hint of green,
Out across the hills and down by the brook,
But it never seems to be there when I wander out to look.
So it's back to the feed wagon to put another bale on
And count the endless hours until a warmer dawn.
Nothing's changed since fall
But the calendar on the wall
And I'm still waiting for this winter to be gone.

When I got up this morning I was still tired and sore
My back started aching before I did my chores.
My joints must be protesting the winter's long run
And waiting for summer to ensure it's done.
I turned the cows out early, much to their dismay
For that's a sure sign that Spring's here to stay.
But the aches haven't left me, no matter what I try
And I'm as cold as those cattle as they give me the eye.
So it's back to the closet to put another shirt on
And count the endless hours until a warmer dawn.

Nothing's changed since fall
But the calendar on the wall
And I'm still waiting for this winter to be gone.

They tell me that my cows, my tractor and my fire
Release some kind of gas that heats the earth up higher
So I guess I better go out and turn them all back on,
'Cause nothing else is working to make this winter gone.

Family Matters

When I was growing up, the vision that I had
Was to run the family business and be just like my dad.
With hard work, a keen mind, and an empty pauper's purse,
He'd become a local legend, but still put family first.
I loved and admired him, and still do to this day,
Despite the thirty years now, since he has passed away.

Where we go in life is a matter of choice and chance,
And mine went a different way because of circumstance.
Over time, my dreams evolved to fit the new reality;
Some of them were realized and some were torn from me.
But clearly now in retrospect, when all is said and done,
The only one that mattered was to be my father's son.

The Hat Makes the Man

When I was growing up
        out on Taylor Flats,
I spent my time
        in a Stetson hat.
It was an Open Road
        in stone-washed gray
And the first thing on
        at the start of every day.
I'd wear that hat
        'til the day was through,
And if I was lucky,
        I'd sleep in it too.

It had a three-finger crease
        in the front of the crown.
With the back rolled up
        and the brim pulled down,
It shaded the sun's glare
        From my eyes
And the four X beaver
        Kept my hair dry.
But between you and me
        the best of the deal
Was the way it looked
        and made me feel.
I felt like a million
        when wearing that hat,
The closest I'd get
        to money like that.

So every time a limb
        caught and sliced it up
Or it was badly treated
        by one of the pups,
I was off to town
        to buy one more
'Til I busted my credit
        at the dry goods store.

By then, I was old
   and a little too fat
To dismount every time
   the wind took my hat.
I saw it as a sign
   that a change was due
And started looking around
   for something new.
I noticed the boys
   across the way
As they planted the crops
   and mowed the hay
They tore up those fields
   without a mishap
Wearing something akin
   to a baseball cap.

When I inquired to see
   what the cost might be
I heard the seed store
   was providing them for free.
Now that was a price
   even I could afford
So I made my way
   into that seed store.
Only to learn
   the price of free
Was a slogan that read
   "I've gone to seed."

That was too close
   to my reality
So I went to the bin
   that wasn't for free.
There I found a variety
   of fabrics and hues,
In such great profusion
   That it was hard to choose.
But I remembered an adage
   I'd learned in my youth:
When in doubt, the best bet
   is the simple truth.

So I bought me a cap;
        that was inscribed to say:
"My horse ate my Stetson
        when I couldn't buy hay."

Over time I noticed
        folks believed what they read
When they saw it displayed
        on top of my head.
It came to me then
        as if from on high
As I raced to the store
        for my one final buy

The slogan for the hat
        to be buried in.
"Forgive me cause I'm too broke
        to pay for my sins."

When The Breeze Becomes A Storm

He was climbing a ridge
And half way there,
When he caught the smell
Of rain in the air.

That and the clouds
Gathering in the skies
Suggested he might
Want to compromise.

He could always return
On some other day,
But he hated for Nature
To have her own way.

The other gender
Had always bested him
And just this once,
He wanted to win.

He'd outlasted blizzards
And a flash flood or two
He just hunkered down
And rode them on through.

Just when he'd decided
It might pass him by,
A thunderous boom
Rolled through the sky.

He feigned disregard,
But just in case,
Prompted the mare
To pick up her pace.

She disagreed
And argued with the bit,
But he couldn't let a wind
Force him to quit.

So he turned her back
And gave her some spur,
And she settled down,
Though she didn't concur.

They were well back in
With no shelter near,
And the weather was fickle
At that time of year.

A little rain was welcome
For the green it would bring,
But snow or a downpour
Were quite different things.

He knew as the sky
Became gun-metal gray,
Both he and the weather
Were headed the wrong way.

But he kept on going,
In groundless belief
That any discomfort
Would likely be brief.

He dropped to the timber
Along the east side
For temporary shelter,
As he continued to ride.

Too set in his ways
To stop or turn back,
He lowered his head
And followed the track.

The wind in the distance
Approached like a train,
Snapping off tree tops
It scattered like rain.

Then everything darkened
In a mist like a shroud,
As buckets of rain
Poured out of the clouds.

A lightning bolt struck
A naked outcrop
And boulders rained down
Like giant rain drops.

By then the mare
Had found the next gear,
As she dashed up the trail,
Her eyes white with fear.

When a massive pine tree
Crashed at their feet,
He had to concede
It was time for retreat.

So he turned for the rim
Where a ledge like a fan
Made a shelter as big
As a horse and a man.

He eased her in
From out of the rain,
And filled his hat
With a handful of grain.

Her withers were shaking
But she calmed right down,
Eating all of the oats
And a little of the crown.

She moved in closer
With each thunder clap,
Until near the end
She was right in his lap.

He knew she'd been right,
So he didn't complain;
He should have turned back
At the first hint of rain.

Hugging himself
To fight off the shakes,
He thought how the day
Was like all his mistakes.

His intellect seemed
To have too soft a voice
So emotion trumped logic,
When it came to a choice.

Always the optimist
When clouds began to form,
He never saw a breeze
As the start of a Storm.

So there they were, cold
And hungry and stiff
Fending off Nature
At the base of a cliff.

Like all things, it passed
But not for a while,
So to warm up his legs
He walked the first mile.

As he mounted back up
He said with a grin:
"Next time old girl,
I'll let you win."

But she knew for certain,
That just like before;
The next wind was a breeze
And nothing more.

He'd downplay the signs,
He'd prevaricate,
Only turning to her
After it was too late.

That's just how it was
For she'd known from the start
That like every other cowboy,
He led with his heart.

Turning Out

Eventually the inversion breaks
And the air is crisp and clean.
In the sunny days that follow,
The hills are blushing green.
The stream is overflowing,
The water far from clear,
As patches of snow up in the norths
Slowly disappear.

The buds nearly opened,
Are refusing to unfold,
As long as starry nights
Make mornings bitter cold.
A lone wildflower emerges,
As spring's first envoy,
In a crown of dew drops
Like sparkling tears of joy.

And the sky is filled with music
Where the geese and sandhill cranes
Make the passage northward,
While the winter weather wanes.
It's still a little early
In these parts here about,
But soon, very soon,
Will be time for turning out.

Throughout the prolonged winter
We've met our livestock's needs,
Breaking ice on the pond
And spreading out their feed.
The days were all dictated
By the work being done,
But a happy end's in sight
With the coming of the sun.

The calves are on the ground
Their noses warm and dry
And the cows no longer bellow
When the feed truck passes by.

They find enough new growth about
To wean themselves from hay
And know they'll soon be grazing
In meadows far away.

Now the days are long enough
For the cycle to begin
And when the days grow shorter
We'll bring them home again.
All summer in the mountains,
As they amble all about
We'll enjoy the freedom
Of having turned them out

The kids are doing chores
Out in the implement yard
And despite all the laughter
I know they're working hard.
It wasn't long ago
Like new calves in the sun
They'd run and butt their heads
While little work got done.

But now all that has changed
And it seems to me of late
There isn't any question,
They're pulling their own weight.
It's not their strength or size,
But how they manage things;
The way they seem to handle
Whatever fortune brings,
Makes me melancholy,
For it leaves me little doubt
That soon, very soon,
Will be time for turning out.

While turning out's a blessing,
It can also be a curse.
Things happen in the forest
That we cannot reverse.

Sometimes a hungry predator
Takes one for its prey
Sometimes one's misguided
And gets lost along the way.

We must hope with our labors
To mark the path so clear
That they, like those before them,
Will find their way back here.
The ruckus in the pasture
Will tell the bottom line;
They're back where they belong,
And they turned out just fine.

The Perfect Ten

I'm not sure why, but it is a simple truth
That my body's unaccompanied by its former youth,
Leaving me alone to contend
With a back and knees that just don't bend.
In this condition, I should concede
To buy all the equipment that I need
To work the ranch with relative ease,
But that's not possible in times like these.
So I rely on resources I have at hand;
I call my son when it's time to brand.
He calls some folks that he's befriended
To see if last year's wounds have mended.
When we have enough to make a go,
We schedule this year's rodeo.

Now old timers might be offended
At how we get a calf upended;
But it works and when we're done
We've usually managed to have some fun.
I go in first with my lariat
For the head or heals, whatever I can get.
The boys then latch onto the line
Adding their collective weight to mine.
Thus the small calves are quickly subdued,
But the larger ones can be just plain rude.
You'd think you'd roped a full grown cow
As they drag us around like a cowboy plow,
Digging furrows and cutting roots
With all those fancy pointy-toed boots.
We plant enough boys for a bumper crop
But eventually, the chaos stops.
Then whoever's turn has come around
Is expected to throw that calf to the ground.
The others stand back to give critique
And up to ten points for the best technique.

Calves should be small when we commence,
But this year the bull had jumped the fence.
So by the time we had enough dry ground,
Calves outweighed cowboys by several pounds.

We started small and things went great,
So I rewarded the cowboys with solid eights,
Before turning next to a slender lad
Whose luck it seemed had just gone bad.
He drew the oldest of the brood,
Built like a brick with an attitude.

When the calf rushed out on the dead run,
My throw for its heels only caught one.
It kept on going 'til the rope got tight
And launched this cowboy like a kite.
My son was able to grab my shirt
And finally wrestle me down to the dirt.
About then I heard an eager yelp
As my dog decided I could use some help.
But her presence failed to instill any fear,
It just kicked that calf into another gear.
We dug in as the calf pulled back.
Then suddenly the rope went slack,
Clearly signaling to my dismay
It was going to fight, not run away.

With its head down around our shins,
It scattered us like bowling pins.
I was the only one left standing there,
'Til it came back to pick up the spare.
For that act of spite the price was dear,
And eventually made that bull a steer.
'Cause that final charge went right over Slim
Who reached up and pulled it down on him.
Arms and legs were so intertwined
What belonged to whom couldn't be divined.
So to prevent the calf from making another run
We hog tied them both until the job was done.

Then we turned them back into the pen
And I awarded that calf a perfect ten.

Eventide

Eventide

Committed to task, I often drive on,
And miss the beauty of the breaking dawn,
What with dogged pursuit of myriad chores
That inevitably seem to generate more.
As each new straw is added to the stack
It tightens the pegs on the strings of my back.
Just when I think they are ready to fray,
I am relieved to see it's the end of the day.

When the chaos of life is set aside
And I give myself over to the eventide.

At one time, I thought in retrospect
That payment was dear for my hasty neglect.
But the passage of time has made it clearer
That morning is eventide seen in the mirror.
The stillness and hues, no better or worse,
Their roles the same, just played in reverse.
Eventually I saw where the problem lay:
There's no sense of fulfillment to start the day.

So instead of regretting the path untried,
I treasure what's left of my eventide.

The fading rays of the waning sun
Rise from the hills when the day is done.
Their pastel colors warm and bright
Forestall the chill of the coming night.
To pay for fatigue from the day now spent
They offer the glow of self content.
Inhaling the stillness of the desert air,
I think of the fruit my labors bear,

My aches are transformed to points of pride
That buoy my spirits in the eventide.

I replay in my mind the day's events
Archiving those of consequence.
The rest I leave to join their peers,
As the flotsam and jetsam of all my years.

I release my tensions, one at a time
Not knowing the reason, let alone the rhyme
For having carried them throughout the day
And taking so long to put them away.

No matter now, for I've hit my stride
And I'm feeling the peace of eventide.

The harder my day has been to endure
The sooner I long for the evening's allure.
The promise of reflection and quietude
Strengthen my resolve and lighten my mood.
For evening's a gift that is unsurpassed,
Perhaps because it does not last.
It's a stop on the way between light and dark
Where we prepare ourselves to disembark

On the journey to night and all that's implied
In going beyond the eventide.

Will There Be Fences In Heaven

I stare into the embers by the fireside,
Wondering what I'll need for my last big ride.
A lifetime of wrangling, has helped me understand
You have to be prepared if you want to be top hand.
And I've little to show after working all these years;
I'm long on experience and short on gear.

So I wonder;
Will there be chores after this life, like haying and rounding up strays?
Or will I need a brand new saddle for riding round Heaven all day?
Is it open range in Heaven, if that should be my fate?
I'm too old to dismount a tall horse just to open a gate.
And who shoes all of those horses? Who rakes and mucks the stalls?
Am I going there to care for the righteous, or to answer my very own call?

Will there be fences in Heaven?
Do they build them high and stout?
And what are their intentions;
Will they keep me in or out?
I need answers to my questions before the final bell.
Cause if I'm not ready for Heaven, then I might as well go to Hell.

And I wonder:
Does the Devil brand his own cattle? Do they stoke those fires hot?
Will I need a pair of new gloves, or can I get by with the ones that I've got?
Are the pastures grass or ashes? Do they stretch the wires tight?
Should I get a brand new bedroll, or will I work right through the night?
Do they gamble in Satan's parlor? Do they drink and fight, and swear?
And where is it that they send you, if you're caught misbehaving down there?

Are the trails very long in Heaven; do they make them double wide?
Should I be heading out early, or can we travel side by side?
I guess I should've paid more attention to choices given to me,
That I might be better equipped to face my own destiny.
Now maybe there's still time enough to remove some of this doubt.
If I hang around earth a while longer and try to sort it all out.

Brandy

There is a photograph that hangs above my fireplace
Of a big red Irish setter, with a wide smile on her face;
And though she has been gone now for far too many years,
Every time I see that picture, it fills my eyes with tears.
Brandy was the first dog I could ever call my own.
She turned my world right over the day I brought her home.
I taught her how to hunt and heel; she taught me how to play.
We were inseparable until nine months from that day,
When the first of my two children, a bouncing baby girl,
Knocked me off the pedestal in the center of that dog's world.
She was their playmate and their pony, their buddy and
bodyguard.
And when the children played outside, she was the fence
around the yard.
In Brandy's mind, they were hers, my daughter and my son;
And when it came to big red dogs, every family needed one.

Her coat of long, fine, silky hair was never quite the same
After bubblegum and cockle burrs from chasing kids and
game.
Her nose once so effective at staying on a track
Was lost in nightly battles with the skunks that lived out
back.
There was many a fascination between the house and school
bus bend,
But she led them there each day and safely back again.
Behind those sad and loving eyes, there ran a special clock
That had her waiting patiently, each day at their bus stop.
Even when infirmities left her half deaf and blind,
She made it up the hill each time and left no child behind.
She was their playmate and their pony, their buddy and
bodyguard.
When the children played outside, she was the fence around
the yard.
No matter what the task was, be it work or just for fun,
When it came to big red dogs, every family needed one.

While her memory is immortal, her life was short at best.
It rained that day in the desert as she found her final rest.
I placed her on the river shore neath the roses where she played;
So it was a dad not a dog that brought the children home that day.
Now it's with a smile and a tear that I look across the yard
To where the rose is brighter still and she stands eternal guard.
Of this I am quite certain, when life's cycle is complete,
I'll return to grassy meadows with Brandy at my feet.
We'll catalogue adventures as far as we can roam,
Then find a place to faithfully wait the children's last trip home.
She'll be their playmate and their pony, their buddy and bodyguard.
And when they try to wander, she'll be the fence around the yard.
For time has clearly proven, when all is said and done,
When it comes to big red dogs, even heaven will need one.

Dearest Mother

"Neath the wispy halo of her snowy white hair
She holds forth daily upon her rocking chair.
Where the rhythm of her motion, like a metronome,
Counts out the days until she turns for home.
She feels the comforting warmth that all her memories give
Rocking through the twilight years of a life that was well
lived.
And though her body's weakened, there is strength at its core
Strength she still provides to the children that she bore.

Her world seems quieter with each passing day,
Even when the newscast is turned up all the way.
Yet she seems to hear the pleas when others need her aid,
And her purse is just enough for a difference to be made.
In the struggle to withstand an ever present chill,
The furnace is on high, despite the power bill
But her heart is even warmer and reaches to the truth
That lies beyond the hardship that lingers from her youth.

The chores are still performed, the house is neat and clean
And very little changes in what is now routine.
The walls are covered with pictures, the gardens teem with
flowers,
And every day she has three meals served upon the hour.
The photos on the mantel move closer to the rim,
Every time the family tree adds another limb.
And each child is cherished for being who they are.
So when they fly off from the nest, their hearts don't go too
far.

Dearest Mother, may I sit beside your chair
For the love and wisdom in the stories that you share?
If I can learn from them, when I'm in your place
I'll look back contentedly on a life of gentle grace.

Homeward Bound

I walked these woods once before;
I climbed the hills and trees.
I slept out in the meadows,
And I sheltered in the lees.

It was a wondrous place,
But that was lost on me,
For I was just passing through
On the road to maturity.

I was so committed
To my journey's end
That I rushed ahead to see
What lay around each bend.

By keeping my eyes forward,
Never stopping to look back,
I failed to see there were no lines
Between fantasy and fact.

There were creatures in these woods.
Some fearsome, some benign.
And their noises in the dark
Scared me at the time.

I never sorted out,
Which was friend and foe.
So I kept them well behind me,
And now I still don't know.

But I suspect I was wrong,
And I will come to find
There was more to fear ahead,
Than all that lay behind.

So now it is with relish
That I turn about
To listen to the sounds
And try to sort them out.

The woods seemed bigger then,
But now I know this truth;
The distance had been stretched
By impatience in my youth.

I thought when I emerged
I'd be fully grown,
And I would know everything
That needed to be known.

But I overlooked too much
That I was meant to find.
So I hope to now retrieve
Those things I left behind.

I know that I must hasten
To make this last chance good,
For there is little time left:
Home lies just beyond the wood.

I am starting to recall
Those forgotten sights and sounds
As I feel beneath my feet
Once familiar ground.

If life is a circle,
Mine is coming round.
And it won't be long now,
Before I'm homeward bound.

I'm Over The Top*

I'm over the top and feeling the pain
Of going downhill on a runaway train
The faster it goes, the slower I get
Soon I'll be still, but I'm not there just yet.

It was a surprise to see in the mirror
A portrait of me after too many years,
With the lines on my face and the gray in my beard.
I looked like the man that I've always feared.
I was saddened to note what I took to be
Both fright and regret staring back at me.
But a second look revealed an inner light
That suggested the first time, I didn't get it right.
The case may be battered, its provenance impugned
But the fiddle inside still carries a tune.
The beat may be slower, the style somewhat dated,
But the love of the music has never been sated.
Oh sure, in the morning I'm stiff and I'm sore,
And my joints aren't as nimble as they were before;
But a little sunshine goes a long way
In warming me up, so I'm ready to play.
I tighten the pegs and rosin the bow,
Then there's nothing better than letting it all go.
My songbook's old, and so am I,
But when I hear new licks, I give them a try.
These arthritic fingers may miss a few notes,
But there's plenty of passion with every bow stroke.
So I'll keep on playing when I get the chance
Because I'm not leaving 'til the end of this dance.

I'm over the top and feeling the pain
Of going downhill on a runaway train
The faster it goes, the slower I get,
But the best of my tunes haven't come yet.

*Carmen and Dick Gilman have turned this into a wonderful
duet.

John Riley's Boys

John Riley's boys were lean and spare
Neath freckled cheeks and auburn hair;
With tempers that were quick to rise
Came winning smiles and laughing eyes.
A Celtic Blend of arms and art
A poet's tongue, a warrior's heart,
They harbored something deep inside
That made them go all misty-eyed.
And at those times, t'was known to friends
The boys were back in Ireland.

John Riley's boys were first to cheer
When James Polk called for volunteers
To push the borders to the sea
Where lay the nation's destiny;
But Yankee soldiers took it hard,
Held Irish lads in low regard.
Disdained with no apology
Their Catholic-based theology.
The boys held out until the end
By remembering their Ireland.

St. Patrick's soldiers one by one,
Sailed off into the setting sun,
To start anew across the sea
And chase the dream of living free.
But things are ne'er what they seem
And Irish souls are evergreen.

John Riley's boys were filled with shame
When marching orders finally came.
Poor peasants 'neath the tyrant's boot
Would take the brunt of this dispute.
'Twas Mexico they would invade,
To fight their namesake's own brigade
In defiance of a mighty host,

The Irish up and left their posts.
And few who saw could comprehend,
The boys recalled old Ireland.

John Riley's boys were mortified
When forced to take the invader's side.
When made to choose with whom they stood,
They chose their souls o'r nationhood.
They fought to their last cap and ball,
Then Winfield Scott said hang them all.
No Irish jig the gallows dance,
Just tragic end to circumstance
And all who saw it did contend
The boys had swung for Ireland.

St. Patrick's soldiers one by one,
Returned into the rising sun
To rest there in eternity
Unfairly scorned, but finally free
Not the future they'd foreseen,
But Irish souls are evergreen.

Longing

There's something about the mountains that sets my
heartstrings free;
They break the common shackles that restrain the wild in
me.
Maybe it's the crisp, clear air, as sharp as a surgeon's blade
Or the shimmer of the wildflowers as they grace the forest
glade;
Maybe it's the rushing water laughing merrily
As it cuts the peaks to grains of sand for burial at sea;
And maybe it's the way they seem to float above the plain;
That lures me into longing for the things I can't explain.

At times when I am set adrift from all that anchors me
(The comfort of familiar things, the dreams of what can't be),
There is a fissure in my chest; a crater opens wide
And everything I thought secure, seems now to me denied.
I gaze into the distance where the horizon used to be
Longing for the mountains, but they're too far for me to see.
I know if there is hope at all to restore my heart and soul,
Only the mountains are big enough to fill the gaping hole.

The Memory Shed

I was but half done
With a very long day
And already dog tired
From bucking wet hay.

So I lay on some straw
Enjoying the shade
Inside an outbuilding
My ancestors had made.

I gazed at the roof
Where the sunlight streamed,
Through rafters made
From hand-hewn beams.

They were twenty foot long
And twelve inches wide,
With the tracks of an adze
Clearly etched on each side.

The ends had been tapered
And neatly dove-tailed
So they'd stay in place
Without peg or nail.

Each truss was heart wood
From back in the day
When pine filled the meadows
Where we cut our hay.

As I scanned their length,
I noted with pride
The initials engraved
On the undersides.

Like the records
Found in a church registry
They proclaimed the branches
Of my family tree.

I could see the trolley
On its iron rail
that shuttled the hay
Before we had bales.

And I know from my youth
That somewhere back there
Were the scraps and twigs
Of a pack rat's lair.

About then I saw
Peering down from his keep
The current tenant
I'd aroused from his sleep.

His anthracite eyes
Had volumes to say,
As he sized me up
Then went on his way.

I felt a connection
Since I knew that his line
Had been living up there
For as long as mine.

And I am quite certain
He boasted a décor
Of the shiny objects
He'd found on the floor.

He probably had the conch
That vanished from sight
When Grandpa left his saddle
On the ground one night.

Rings from old harnesses
And ribbons from pails
Are no doubt mixed in
With spare horseshoe nails.

But there were more displays
Than that pack rat's nest
In this Museum's exhibit
Of the Wild, Wild West.

Even the siding
Had tales to tell
Like the pellets imbedded
From a shotgun shell.

And the slap dash patch
About six feet tall
Where I'd driven a tractor
Right through the wall.

Seems everywhere I turned
There was something of note
That sparked a memory
Or a lump in my throat.

Wherever boards met
A quick scan would show
The history of fasteners
From a century ago.

All manner of screws
And lag bolts were found
With evolution of the nail
From square head to round.

So, too, the boards
On the sides and the loft,
With rough cut and milled,
Beside hardwood and soft.

About then I heard
Old John Deere cough
And scrambled to board,
Before they took off.

I hopped on the wagon
And sat in the back
Looking at that building
As we chugged up the track.

I couldn't stop smiling
As it dawned on me
That to others it looked
Quite differently.

When passers-by saw it
All weathered and gray,
With disparate patches
Where boards broke away,

They no doubt believed
We didn't give a darn,
For they mistakenly thought
It was just an old barn.

The Prairies of the Sky

About a block off Main Street
Where the houses need new stain
He'd commandeered a rocking chair
And stared out at the rain.
There was a sadness in his eyes
And chiseled in his cheeks
Were lines like rugged canyons
That carry mountain creeks.
Stoic as he looked at first,
He suddenly seemed frail
When a fit of coughing
Had him struggling to inhale.
I offered him assistance,
Said it was warm inside;
But he just shook his head,
And eventually replied:

"I'm ready for the leaving,
I've packed up all my things.
I just pray my baggage
Isn't too much for some wings.
This world is far too crowded
Since they plowed the plains
If I don't jump those fences
I might go insane.
I'm hoping there's a place
Where the wires aren't so high,
For I'm eager to be riding through
The prairies of the sky."

I nodded, but said nothing
To me it was quite plain
His fears had come to pass;
He was no longer sane.
For all the prairies now
Are fields of corn and grain
And clouds ride the sky
Along with birds and planes.

But I maintained my silence
For though I had the means,
It's not within my nature
To dash another's dreams.

It wasn't but a week or two
I found myself back there
And heard the boards complaining
Beneath that rocking chair.
But it wasn't that old cowboy,
Behind the mournful sound;
A day or two before that
They had laid him in the ground.
I tarried there a moment
As the chair rocked in the wind
Fearing that it was a sign
Of a spirit still fenced in.
Then lightening flashed above me,
As a dark cloud skittered by.
And I heard a cattle call
Chase it across the sky.
I couldn't keep from smiling
As I turned away.
(I wonder how a cloud responds
To yippee yi kayay?)

And then it dawned on me,
The deeper message there:
That answers can be found
For each and every prayer.
Because the clouds change shape
As on their way they fly,
Anything can happen
In the prairies of the sky.

The Silent Hills

There's an old skidder rusting out by the spruce,
Its fenders bent and battered, its wires hanging loose.
The choker cable on the back has seen far better days,
There's little pull left in it, the way the strands are frayed.
Climbing spikes and a safety belt lie in the nearby shed,
Beneath a singing whip that hangs from overhead.
Its music but a memory to those long since disbanded,
The ones that ran the green chain when saw wood was
demanded.

The silhouette upon the wall stands out in contrast clear
Where caulked boots have been hanging, for lo these many
years.
As dark as recent times have been, enough sunlight got
through
To fade the paint around them and crack their leather, too.
Off to the side there is a pair of faded dungarees
With the hems removed to free them from limbs on fallen
trees.
An old tin hat and braces hooked up there with the pants
Complete this silent prayer to the God of one last chance.

For over a hundred years now past, the long line of his kin
Felled giant trees with axes for the horses to bring in.
He listened to his grandpa's tales and sat in wondrous awe
Of two-man teams out cutting trees using twelve-foot saws,
And with a sense of reverence, he also heard the pain
In how the mighty blades gave way to modern moving chains.
Then suffered when the logging crews grew both few and small
Until the fateful day came when there was no work at all.

With empty eyes and an empty heart he sits out on the porch
Wondering if someone else will come to carry on the torch.
He walks the streams and woodlands to find his simple fare,
Thankful for the bounty that Nature's left him there.
But those brief trips are bitter sweet, as he passes through
the trees
And sees the homes and buildings that surely they should be.
Then thunderstorms make a fiery track through the silent hills
And all the logs go up in smoke that should be in the mills.

There is a battle raging in the northern lands:
Whether to cut trees or to let them stand.
Some folks say that their peace of mind
Is well worth a logger in a welfare line.
Happy to put a tin cup in his hand,
God have mercy on the timber man.
May God have mercy on a timber man.

The Painting

The easel stands by the window, angled to catch the light
On a sheet of untouched canvas that is agonizingly white.
The emptiness reaches out to me to capture the perfect thought,
But despite its good intentions, nothing has been caught.
A clutch of brushes in the tray, their bristles clean and dry
Look longingly at the palette and the oil tubes set nearby.
Photographs and remembrances lay strewn about the place
In hopes of inspiring images that could fill the empty space.
But nothing there emerges; the void remains the same.
So I step back from the room, and the door becomes a frame,
I sign my name as artist, and affix the title thereon:

"Still life, after the muse is gone?"

Give The Horse His Head

In the seeming eternity since he'd become bed bound
He hadn't moved an extremity nor uttered a single sound.
He lay trapped in a useless body, white as the sheets he wore,
With tubes and wires connected to an entire hardware store.
Electronic beeps and blinking lights cluttered up the air,
And helped to fill the void in what were now just empty chairs.

Gone were the visitors, locked in hushed debate
Discussing all his options in light of faith and fate.
Daily in their place he heard a different voice instead
That whispered in his ear: "Just give the horse his head.
You've worked hard all your life, Jim. Your earthly chores are done.
Just drop the reins and lean way back and let that pony run.
What seemed so great a journey is not far from this bed.
The endless plain awaits you, Jim. Just give the horse his head."

He couldn't remember what happened, let alone the cause;
But he had a notion it confirmed the first of Murphy's Laws.
He was sure there'd have been a horse, so the irony was clear
Each time the voice came visiting and whispered in his ear.
More importantly it seemed, he held the feelings of his friends
When they concluded only God determines when it ends.
So he clung to that slippery slope above the great abyss
And prayed there was some higher good that justified all this.
He steeled his nerve and waited, filled with quiet dread,
While fending off that nagging voice: "Just give the horse his head.
What purpose could there be now to enduring all this pain?
Who could ever fault you now for letting loose the reins?
What others think so noble, is stubbornness instead.
The endless plain awaits you, Jim. Just give the horse his head."

His lonely circumstances gave him time to contemplate
Issues that would normally have carried too much weight.
And in those times he wondered to what end he clung so tight,
For there was nothing he could do to set his past wrongs right.

If his future was eternal fire to pay for going astray,
The present differed little from the future he delayed
Holding on would buy some time, not change the destination.
Yet he would suffer even more in anxious anticipation.
Once he realized the time he bought was relatively brief,
He was reconciled unto himself and joy replaced his grief.
The comfort of the notion then let him loose his grip
And feel the stallion surge, as the reins began to slip.
The wind was in his face, as his mortal shell he shed
And freedom was upon him as he gave the horse its head.

Cassie

I've had Cassie 15 years now, ever since she was a pup,
So it comes as no surprise, she's having trouble keeping up.
But I can still remember when she raced ahead each day
Then turned back to assure herself that I'd not lost my way.
Sometimes she'd retrace her steps until I came in view
Then bark at me as if to say: "Hurry up, we've things to do."
Then dashing off she'd go again and the bawling let me know
The herd was trailing nicely with the stragglers well in tow.

Clouds now linger in those eyes that used to brightly shine
And there's little doubt about it that her hearing's worse than mine.
If I call her from the east side, she's quickly western bound
And there's hitches in her joints whenever she gets up or down.
Sleeping is her full time job; she's a master of the trade,
But I know that she still dreams of every cattle drive we made.
Her muscles flex and twitch with every dodge and leap,
And not a single cow is lost, although she's sound asleep.
I see her in my mind's eye, as that youthful red merle streak
And have to turn aside to hide the dampness on my cheek.

I know I don't have long now, as her waking hours are few;
Prudence says to get another, before her time is through.
But I haven't got it in my heart to break hers at the end;
She isn't just a cow dog; she's my shadow and my friend.
I do not know what I will do, the time she doesn't wake
I see her running out ahead, then stopping for my sake.
She'll wonder what's become of me and why I don't respond
As she barks and wags her tail from the hilltop just beyond.
So I sit down right beside her now, and close my eyes to see
If there's a better way for partners like my Cassie dog and me.

Winter Is Coming*

Autumn came early and to my surprise.
At the first hint of morning, I opened my eyes
To see snow on the mountain and geese in the skies,
So I leaned out the window to hear their goodbyes.
Their voices are many, yet they strive as one,
To hold back time, by chasing the sun.
But try as they might, there'll be no delay,
Darkness and cold are heading this way,
For winter is coming, come what may.

I hear the sounds of an arctic breeze
Down by the river in the maple trees
Chasing their sap as it bends them with ease,
It batters their limbs and strips them of leaves.
Once fallen, leaves scatter like mice in a maze,
Seeking a refuge to lengthen their stay.
But try as they might, there'll be no delay,
Darkness and cold are heading this way,
For winter is coming, come what may.

The ice on the pond is as gray as a stone
It imprisons the water as if to atone
For the pleasures of summer long since flown
And the chill in the air is now deep in my bones.
The lengthening shadows quickly defeat
The unbridled hope that was morning's conceit.
Evening like autumn makes ready the way
For darkness and cold to complete our day,
And winter is coming us, come what may.

This morning's sky is no longer blue,
But white as the frost that was yesterday's dew.
And the hours that are left are far too few
To change the course by starting anew,
It all seemed so simple when I first embarked,
But the journey is long and the route is unmarked
Try as I might, I can't seem to delay
The rapid approach to the end of my day
For winter is coming, come what may.

*This poem has been put to music.

128

Goodbye

I wept all night in solitude,
My heart was torn in two
When I could not assemble US
Without the missing U.
Perhaps it had been taken
To make our last adieu.

LaVergne, TN USA
09 September 2010
196507LV00001B/1/P